the barman

Also by John Lancaster

Effects of War Giant Steps Press 1986
Split Shift (with Geoff Hattersley) Smith/Doorstop 1990

Acknowledgements

Thanks to the editors of the following magazines in which the poems listed have appeared:

Ambit (Cabbages; Missionary; A Flood)
Encounter (Pure Research)
Iron (Waking Up; The Usherette)
London Magazine (Occupational Therapy; A Curse For The Man Who Came To Dinner; The Gospel Tent, New Orleans Jazzfest, 1978)
Orbis (At The Corner Table)
Slow Dancer (Hang Down Your Head Tom Dooley; Woman's Hours; In The Breaks Between Bingo; The Boy In You; Lights Which Don't Go Out; The Barman III)
Verse (For The Secret; The Queer)
Scratch (Are Made Of This; The Barman VII and VIII)
The North (Cabbages)
The Rialto (At Holkham Beach, Norfolk)
The Echo Room (Building The Palace Of Dreams)
The Wide Skirt (The Barman I and XVII; Sicilian Buttercups; ZennybodyevertoldyayalooklikeElvisPresley; T.S. Eliot Gets An Idea; The Longing; Stamps)

the barman
John Lancaster

Smith/Doorstop Books

Published 1993 by
Smith/Doorstop Books
The Poetry Business
51 Byram Arcade
Westgate
Huddersfield HD1 1ND

Copyright © John Lancaster 1993
All rights reserved

ISBN 1 869961 39 0

Typeset at The Poetry Business
Printed by Walkers Printers, Clayton West, Huddersfield
Distributors: Password (Books) Ltd., 23 New Mount Street, Manchester
M4 4DE

The Poetry Business gratefully acknowledges the help of Kirklees
Metropolitan Council and Yorkshire & Humberside Arts.

Contents

Part I
7 - 30 The Barman (I - XVII)

Part II
33 Cabbages
34 T.S. Eliot Gets An Idea
35 At Holkham Beach, Norfolk
36 At The Corner Table
37 For The Secret
38 Hang Down Your Head Tom Dooley
40 The Queer
41 Woman's Hours
42 Boon and Mills
44 Murdo
45 Life Class
46 A Flood
47 Missionary
48 Soutine
50 Sicilian Buttercups
51 Pure Research
52 ZennybodyevertoldyayalooklikeElvisPresley
53 The Boy In You
      1. Waking Up 53
      2. The Boy In You 53
      3. Past Present 54
      4. Dick 55
56 Building The Palace Of Dreams
57 After The Fight At The Picket
59 Repetition Is The Death Of Us They Say
60 The Longing
61 The Gospel Tent, New Orleans Jazzfest, 1978
62 Are Made Of This
63 The Usherette
64 A Cure For The Man Who Came To Dinner
65 Occupational Therapy
66 In The Breaks Between Bingo
67 Lights Which Don't Go Out
68 The Wire-Coathanger Story
70 Stamps

Part I

THE BARMAN

(I — XVII)

My thanks to American writer Jo Smalley whose unpublished short story 'Homeless' gave me the idea for 'The Barman' and from which quotations are made in the first and last poems of the sequence.

I

At six, they crowded in from battered Transits,
powerless except for what they could do on a site,
their only hope in talk. He had been there —
talking of the pub at work, of work in the pub.
And as they warmed with this routine, he wondered,
does it really matter on which donkey dreams
we pin our tails? The next second-hand car to be the one
that won't break down; the lucky break; the going home
for good? All this in these, the stuck and restless
with return to sender stamped in their eyes. Yet
sometimes when they spoke it reminded him of opening
old paperbacks, how dust flew out like tiny butterflies,
surprised you; their shocking bits of sense. Through these
he found connections and something infinite in the history
of strangers. But as the night grew, all they wanted
was to see how far they could ride the memories, exile's
vicious freedom. No one dared give the juke box the kick
that would release them from replaying *The Wild Rover*
over and over. At time, they spoke freely of keeping
promises to dying mothers and of moments of choking sadness
when watching families in supermarkets while for them
everything midased into shit. Listening, he wondered
who he was, calmly watching the blind ghost inside them
stumble around in the darkness then stop to torture
each of them in turn, some to say they were lost, some
to say they liked it here, some to say it could be worse,
all in the monotone of the migratory loops which the English
programmed, planted in their heads those years ago.
And afterwards, they soothed it with a rosary of names
of places where everyone knew them, somebody loved them
and men sat on top of poles for days at annual fairs —
Belderrig, Cahir, Borris in Ossory, Killurin, Cregganbaun —
places from which, they explained, they were made to walk
the rut like real forgotten Gaelic princes past crows
and donkeys and hayfields towards dog-eared, cardboard
silhouettes of English towns which would suck them
like they'd never been sucked. And he knew what they meant.

ll

He blamed Spring for bringing him here,
for ending the snowed-in weeks
on the Yorkshire Moors. When it all melted,
he'd been sacked for helping himself
to too much of the stock and the landlord's wife.
No pay-off, he'd got himself to Leeds and
the first train to where his pocket would take him,
heading south through crocus-lined cuttings
to hide in a city for a change.

In every town, the evening paper led
to hand-written signs of staff required.
Never desperate, he would choose,
only enquire when the ingredients felt right.
He preferred the low-light loser-trap
of bad diet skins and broken-veined noses
where smoking wasn't a problem and
helter-skelter paralytics with matted hair
mixed with shouting pretenders to great causes,
mad ideas and stutterers with letters choking
for air. There had to be faces grim as farmers',
sodden turves but which when the mood changed
could laugh into a sun-dried crack,
people who knew that there were a million ways
of making a living and who had found one way
of surviving, people with some vibration
still going, who could still see a field
to walk through. And there would be people
who looked as if they were just about to scream
at you and those who looked as if you were going
to hit them. And there had to be music among
the graces.
It was music which had pulled him in;
the downward sliding chords of *Stormy Monday*
from the blues band setting up. The Blues Rats.
He liked that name. And the zest of the early evening
Irish *craic*. And the waft of goat curry simmering
somewhere out the back. These things. But above all,

fresh daffodils stuffed in a honey jar on the bar
and on the bedside table in the tiny room above
just big enough to take one holdall.

III

He only envied musicians,

how the sax could zoom
from a dry mouth and
nerves enough to shake
the keys to a rattle
like naked puppets' bones
into a soaring tune
moving heavy-booted navvies
to tap their feet and sway
like scaffolding in a gale,

how they could crust
insecurity, broken marriages
and twelve-hour drives down autobahns
with memories of a hundred affairs
on cruise ships, of making love
under a star-lit bandstand, waking
to find her gone and
camellias inside a horn case.

Best were the Delegates of Pleasure
who'd been to New Orleans,
played parades with Kid Howard
and blues with Billie Pierce,
accompanied strippers on Bourbon Street,
sat in at Luthjen's dancehall,
who played with a beat
that could shift the building
to a higher pulse. Then turn it down,
sweet and low and slow.
Embellishing them

with his own imagination,
he would retell all their stories
wishing they were his
and that he had their talent
to set next to his offerings
of peanuts, pickled eggs
and the skill to change an empty keg.
But what he'd give the most for
was the freedom greater than his own,
how they could blow, give it everything,
then move on, nightly.

Often, after they had left
in a moan of humped speakers
and repair bills for the van,
he would drink alone in a slump,
blame his father for saying no
to trumpet lessons, then bang out
frustration on the old pin-ball table
with its illuminated backboard
of a juggler whose balls
no longer lit up.

IV

There was the Big Day
when the Minister came in
to escape the hostile jeers
after trooping round the burnt-out shops.
The barman remembered how the fine rain
and the smell of riot-smoke
clung to the long, black coat
and the precision with which the sleek head
joined in, pretending to sip a half
with nodding community leaders
while twitchy security men
eyed-up Stephanie, dolled-up
for lunch-time business.
And pouring carefully,
he listened to the words flow,
rise genuine as a pro's climax.
And with the same purpose he thought.

V

Tonight he has Celtic Mary
celebrating a win over Rangers,
just her and her good friend Mr. Teacher
having a hell of a good time.
Zoot, zoot on the optic
and he is waiting for the moment,
usually not long after he's explained
yet again that an atheist is
neither Protestant nor Catholic,
when she will dust off her father,
take away his violence
and put him on an altar.
True, he's a ghost on an outing
based on a man she never met,
the father of a relative
of an old girlfriend
who read stories to her,
kissed her to sleep,
saved up to buy her pretty dresses,
never gave a wage to whores,
never pulled a knife on a mother
one Hogmanay, never walked out
one Christmas.

And he knows she'll go on
until she's done her real thing justice,
converted her picture
into something she never had,
something to worship,
knows that she will always finish
neatly in the cemetery
where people always say the right things.
He hopes that some day,
some match-day night
it will all be different,
that she'll surprise him
with another life, her own.
He likes surprises.

VI

With or without dog collars,
they strut in with their palms held out,
sweet-apple cheeks and glossy lips,
float among without asking his permission
as if this were holy ground
for harassing waverers and backsliders.
They try to clear the clouded vision,
anchor those of drifting hope,
might forgive the unforgiven sins
in return for a friendly stout.
Deep down, he'd like to tell them
to bugger off. But from the sincerity
of the whispered 'yes father' and
the cow-eyed, up-turned faces, it seems
that some folk want, even need it.

VII

He could be resourceful:

> NOTHING HAPPENS
> HERE
> ON MONDAY NIGHT.
> IT'S DEAD AS A DODO.
> SO DON'T BOTHER
> COMING.

He had put the notice in the window
as a last resort after failing
with jazz and stand-up comics,
written it when manic
at the bleep of video games, mindless
at responding to the same three mutes
and grunting at Norman Treacle repeating
Quiet tonight, isn't it?

Being on a bus route, he guessed
that some would come for a joke and
he knew the power of publicity
and perversity. But they packed him out
for three weeks running, some thinking
that dead as a dodo were a rock group,
others waiting for anything to happen.
Run off his feet, he decided he preferred
the old deadliness. But even when he took
the poster down, the momentum of expectancy
and requests for exotic dancers or
Rocky Allen with backing tapes continued.

In desperation, he advertised
a poetry reading.

VIII

Some said you could tell his politics
by those to whom he let the function room —
Sinn Fein, Marxists, Fabians . . .
But he claimed that he had no time for these,
only the regulars who stood for
Them and us and me.
What did they ever do for me?

The long pause which followed this
gave way to a list of answers —
the suddenness of the redundancy letter;
the length of the queue when signing on;
the length of the queue at the hospital;
the wait to replace the stolen giro;
the price of children's shoes . . .

And there were always targets
for these disappointments —
a company director's salary;
a royal granny paid beyond her needs;
a politician being stretchered alive
from the rubble of a bombed hotel . . .
Nothing intellectual, like upstairs.
Just a manifesto of it's only fair,
of right and wrong, of what they wanted,
deserved, had a right to,
what they'd seen done to others,
what they'd had done to themselves,

what they'd like to do to Them.
They would drink to that.
And he would join them.

IX

Billy Hughes had heard the coppers fitting up the Six drinking after hours in the Barrel on Summer Lane: everybody believed him. There was plenty of supporting evidence. Like the night they came in here steamed up and paid for rounds by mentioning the music license application. And they screwed a meal from the Taj Mahal across the road by noticing the license was up for renewal. And they planted grass on Wendell, Audrey the cleaner's lad, when they pulled him on the suss. Round here, everybody had a story — which was the problem with being a barman the barman thought, how the blind-eye and the deaf-ear were supposed to be good qualifications for the job. Hard when you knew the truth. Useless. Powerless. But when they used a deserted corner of the lounge for passing tenners to a grass, he would clear a nearby table slowly, hover, gather information in readiness.

X

When women talked of men,
it was always to replace
what they'd got.
In dinner-time circles,
first they'd ram the crisps and
Coke at bawling baby buggies
slung with Kwik-Save carrier bags
filled with dented tins, then
sank pints of light and bitter
to bloat the gasfire-mottled legs and
fuel a rage where every other word was
bastard.

Then screwing out their fags
in the Guinness ashtray,
they'd burn their rubbish
who hung around the bookies,
went drinking after work
and on to the dogs,
fishing all weekend.

Instead, they wanted,
unreeled their list
of film and telly stars,
what they could do for them.
Now, that Roger Moore . . .

Getting the third round in,
some one would tell him
he looked like Robert Redford.

XI

You never saw them with one
but when men who sat at the bar
talked of women, the women
would all be missing something: them,
best chance they'd ever had.
Somehow they had all met or seen
the one for them
or known a moment they couldn't hold —
a glance across a ballroom;
a conversation at a bus-stop;
a lift they should have taken.

From his own losses,
he could not refuse
this fanning of agony,
would let them repeat beautiful
and Christ you should have seen her,
let them pile up their loves
like tokens saved
for juke-box favourites
whenever the lager would give
their tongues a poise to dance,
release

the chalet maid at Butlin's
with legs up to you know where
and what she could do;
the freckled girl selling blackberries
on a country road in County Clare;
the carrying of Rosemary Nixon's satchel
and swopping school scarf tassels;
the akee seller in Port of Spain.
Even Connemara Patsy who seldom spoke
croaked out his only shudder in a field.
And there was the laughing Pole
who told of an incredible woman
frustrated by her inability
to make him miserable

and how she had left with his wallet
in the middle of the night.
And how he missed her.

As they flicked through
these well-thumbed albums
and years spent on trains,
in bus stations, dancehalls, discos,
but mostly bars,
searching for new faces
to fit these same faces,
he guessed that it was the men
who were missing.
He gave them this
because he knew
you had to be missed
to be missing.

XII

Dettingen, afternoon,
high July

Will this find you? Will it find you
still buried in that place in that city
knowing everybody who comes through the door
and what they'll have, where they'll lean and
rest their foot on the brass rail? Does
the woman in the maroon and gold sari still
drift in looking for her whiskied husband?
Do those pissed Ukrainians still relive
the Second World War every night? Are they
building yet on all the dereliction that
surrounds you? But by now you've surely left
that godawful place. They'll mail this on.
You were always talking of moving, said
everything was quite simple (<u>that</u> simple,
real) Was it true? Is it still? But you
couldn't make this trip. So I wonder if
anyone, anything, anywhere can satisfy,
comfort, calm you.

Well how about this. I am under clouds
like spun sugar, tinted sunset pink
just above the thick-forested horizon. I
am on the balcony and in the orchard below
the local birds have already begun their
evening's songfest. Talk about birds! Here
there are birds for every hour. And there's
a road around the hill that curls past
geometric fields and a few wild,
tall and gloriously old pine trees. There
is a small trickle of a stream and in one
wheat field, a scattering of poppies.
Children ride bikes and wave to me while
I try to draw these lovely clouds. There
are some boys playing football in the yard
below. A farmer is cutting for grain in

*the field across the street. And still
the birds, clouds in heaven and all's right
with the ordinariness of this world right
in front of me.*

*How's that? Does it make the greyness and
the stink of the beer-soaked carpet
any more bearable? Close your eyes
and imagine yourself running through the
forest on the edge of night, sundown
surrounded by trees, stillness and loveliness
of light and sudden birds in the underbrush.
And perhaps me by your side. Better?*

*How are you? It's hard to write from so far
away in space and time. And I'm wondering
too what if anything you want to know about
my life in Konstanz. Actually I don't live
in town but in this tiny village about
a half hour's drive away. To the city I ride
each day to study German, ya. And afternoons
I hang around contemplating the usual, my
destiny and all that. I paint some and today
I'm trying to understand and condense the last
few months of being in motion so that I can
amuse and entertain you with tales of my high
adventures on the continent (that's a tall
order, my adventures have been short in general
and by some standards not adventures at all).*

*Have a beer for me. I've not been drinking much
here (I think I'm here for another month).
Went out to an ancient wine keller the other day —
fine place and the wine was delicious. I talked
French, English, and Spanish and listened to
German (missed a lot but less than I expected).
It's crazy living in this shadowy world where
communication is a continual challenge and/or
constant threat. Adventure of a mild sort.
Enough now for a while. Let me know your new
address. Would like to hear from you. Write from*

where we left off and tell me all the excitement
in your life so that at least I can feel glad
for you. I wish you good weather and good health
and I wait for your letter or you.

love

Patti

He'd shown it to several of us.
Only the rustle of thin airmail paper
broke the silence as it passed along.
Then the communal advice. Everybody
remembered her. A cracker. Green eyes.
Thought she'd stay. Just right for him.
The perfect couple. Never understood
why she'd taken off.

He kept it on a high shelf
rammed down behind a darts trophy,
took it down a lot in the weeks
of bad-tempered mooning. If
anybody asked him what the problem was,
he'd say he was very worried about
using the word bollocks too often.

XIII

Most times there was just the repetition
of the same faces;
of picking losers at Pontefract;
giving change for eight-ball pool;
unjamming the fag machine;
the splitting up of fights
when drunken Ukrainians yelled
that there were Rastafairies
at the bottom of their garden,
or when those not afraid to own their Lord
defended their bit of the Godzone with fists.

When she stepped into it all,
he assumed her silence meant
waiting for someone
or just wanting to drink —
the summer was hot, men wore shorts
for the first time since boyhood
and women halter tops, Bob Marley
owned the juke-box and
Handsworth wanted to drink.
He watched her stroke the glass
and the night heat build its sticky film
on her stillness. And he wondered
what sadness bit into her face
when without having to ask,
suddenly it was said,

how at eighteen she could see it all.
Horses would be important like
from the time when she'd go
and stroke the pony in its stable
when things went wrong, like
her parents fighting. She
would win a rosette, first prize, and
a man in the crowd
would send a message
asking her to dinner.
He would be nearly rich

and say she could go to art school
before they started a family.
They would have four children
and not send them to school. She
would sell her paintings of horses
when not teaching them everything.
Then his business would fail with the times
and in a wild scheme they would all drive
with four mares across Europe, set up
a riding school in Yugoslavia. Five
years of this. Then some fear would grip him.
Back home, no home, moving
from old friend to old friend, he
would start to beat her up
for making the wrong moves.
He would encircle the children,
move her out to a barn across a field
over which he'd send the girls
two days a week. She would survive
by knitting chasers into jerseys.
Returning from a selling trip to London,
she would meet a man on the train
who'd tell her his life story
between Watford and Stoke.
One year he had been to the Derby.
Amazing, she said, how sometimes
the future gallops across your eyes.
The man would meet her here at eight.

As he moved about the bar,
he studied the sadness from different angles,
watched it set and harden as eight
became nine. He tried to imagine
stroking a woman's face that never changes.
And he saw that when you love some one,
you lose something, again and again.

XIV

He catches himself
in the mirror behind the optics,
thinks at least
that he's not cornered,
stuck in this substitute existence
like the men behind him,
men who shatter the silence
rifling dominoes into table tops,
fishermen who abandoned Jamaica,
blue skies and boats,
shivered down Southampton's gangplanks,
thawed out the Fifties
in front of paraffin heaters
in pink and peeling Handsworth rooms,
who here slake the space
between sleep and the night-shift heat
of Smethwick foundries
and in between games count savings
to build
that house on Montego Bay.

Turning to serve the rum,
their talk puts the shell to his own ear.
And of course, as he watches
their sons roar into the night
with shagged-out white girls
in clapped-out Escorts,
it is always him, always him
who'll get out of this place.

XV

Things start changing
when you start comparing
he reckoned, when
the dreary splat of sick
on a tiled floor and
a carrot-blocked basin
reminded him of
the assistant manager's job
at Yates's, Blackpool,
of the man who downed
four pints between orders
and time then threw it back
you never knew where: every
Thursday. Was it that
which made him leave
or the turd coughing out
of a seawall pipe
on a rare day off?
Was it better there than
the high-stooled wine bar
where people pretended
to know red from white, or
the silent Cavalier Steak Bar
where wallet-tough meat
stoppered conversation, or
the Cunt and Trumpet in Bilston
where he barred a man
for leaping over the pumps
and biting the head
off a stuffed pheasant?

It was always this crazy
trailing back among the lounges,
snugs, cellars and faces
which had gone into his life
that would trigger off the itch.
And usually on a fine morning
waiting for the first customer

when an unforecasted sun
drying the mopped floor
would make him notice
the knife-slash
in the new leatherette seating
and that the brilliant white
had turned to nicotine.
And he would think
that he could be picking plums
down Evesham way.
Or pulling cider under thatch
in the Monkey House at Defford.

XVl

Saturday night. Time.
The till done, he smokes,
watching part-time staff
wash glasses, crate empties.
The band still encores.
The crowd rocks, unmovable.
Still hours till bed.
Knackered beyond sleep,
the violence of tiredness grips
and caged
by the locked bar-grille
he stares through,
sees
baboons dancing.

XVll

The man with accusatory eyes
stumbled from the toilets,
trousers down to his ankles,
the unsteady, new-born zebra walk
of modesty left at home.

There's no fuckin' toilet paper in there.

He left the bar,
took the man like a dance partner,
avoided the splattered arse,
twirled him round and
waltzed him back into the gents.
He pushed him across that great divide
to the other stall where
six virgin white rolls waited patiently.
As the door slammed shut,
he read its scrawl:

Wanna have fun on this reckless planet?

And he walked slowly
back to the bar,
finished his shift, quit,
started wandering again.

Part II

CABBAGES

That's what the work-men call us
as we lean on the temporary fence
and watch them build the new extension.
The brickies think it's very funny.
Not understanding it myself,
I got some books from the trolley
they bring around each Thursday.

In *Lessons in Elementary Botany*
by Daniel Oliver F.R.S., F.L.S it says,
'All crucifers (that includes cabbages)
are wholesome and anti-scorbutic.'
By the *Dictionary*, this makes us

healthy and sound,
not shabby, not vile, not mean,
not debilitated, not contemptible.

It makes them wrong in every sense.
But each day they call us cabbages
as we peer beyond their protective fence.

I slip my hand into my friend's
and strolling across the walled-in patch
tell him it's better like this
than to be like that,
that you should lock people up
for being like that

(But who'll believe that I can think
then put all this on paper?)

T.S.ELIOT GETS AN IDEA

Off we go again:
another long one about
civilisation.

AT HOLKHAM BEACH, NORFOLK

Slowed by big survival packs,
as if at altitude or on the moon,
four figures shimmered, plodded
the shore horizon, flawed the layers
of sky on sea on sand on mud.
We saw them stop and read a map
then turn inland, programmed, on course,
defenceless against their orders.

Uncontrolled, the children ran
to print the tide-blanked sand,
yelled and lifted a flock of waders
whose cries, flapping drowned their racket.
They asked us names of plants
which colonise the mud-flats, dunes:
I showed them marram grass,
the only one I know without a book.
Then they found a rusting engine
half-buried now for forty years:
some maybe-U.S. pilot
had not made it from the Ruhr.

The four men passed. Tanned. Fit.
Gaunt. Unsmiling. Louisiana
accents drawled of getting home for fall.
We watched them shrink towards the waiting jeep.
We guessed their bomber would exercise
above the Arctic, rehearsing for our exit.

And we sat and ate and watched the sea-wash
leave its bits of wood and rope and plastic,
said next year they'd need some bigger spades . . .

At the edge of night, we lay and listened
to the constant whisper of the sea cohere
with the children's even breathing:
elemental; what matters; indestructible —
yet vulnerable as everything.
And a jet trained low
with nothing to aim for but the earth's curve.

AT THE CORNER TABLE

He said she looked nice
in the new black outfit.

And they talked about everything
except what he was feeling,

his speech and thought dismembered
like when lying,

his lips refusing to open
out the truth, yet again.

He wished she would say
what he was thinking.

He wished they could be
what the glances thought they were,

that the movement of a hand
would confirm the gossip, loud

like the clacking of dirty plates
from the close kitchen.

Perhaps she was waiting
for the right moment, another time,

was waiting to sort out first
another bit of her life,

that it was too early on
to fly recklessly south.

Or perhaps she saw in his eyes
the fear of one more failure,

saw he thought that if he looked away
to order, she would leave.

FOR THE SECRET

He told me he'd learned
there's no such thing as nearly,

that wanting, imagining, is it -
even if you can't get closer.

To smooth things over, he'd had to say
that nothing had happened with her,

had hidden the ache for a longer day,
a twnty-fifth hour,

when they could slip away unnoticed
from those they loved

to meet and walk with no-one staring,
without need to use the night,

guilt returned to the church from where
it came and small-town fears eclipsed.

Only with her, he told me
he'd learned

it's all behind the eyes,
the shining time.

HANG DOWN YOUR HEAD TOM DOOLEY

Lonnie Donegan. His greatest hit.
But less so than the village version -
Hang down my leg long tooley -
which you heard on Saturdays
in Uncle Frank's black Austin
jammed full of men and boys
on the way to the match.
You learned the words along with

> Women? Trust 'em? Never.
> You're better off in the bathroom
> with a jam jar full of warm liver.

> Give it 'em hard as a rock.
> Never mind their husbands,
> you've got to piss with the cock you've got.

> Get her in her birthday suit
> then slip her on
> like a well-worn old seaboot.

> Get 'em pregnant. Bugger romance.
> When you're halfway up,
> a standing prick's got no conscience.

The smoking Fifties choked you full of all this
and simultaneous equations, Hookes' Law,
parsed sentences, irregular verbs
and *Nod* by Walter de la Mare.
Constrained, tight in your uniform,
you learned it by repetition
or picked it up like thrown rubbish to store
until some yes or no day
some crazy scramble for sense day
I can see it all day
this is what I think day
I have got it right day

when your knackered, scrubbing mother became
woman doing everything bar bringing the money in
and there was language beyond the parish boundary
when Beckett's *All That Fall* and Aneurin Bevan
crackled from the wireless. And you read
there was something in London called
Look Back In Anger. And you fell out for ever
with the other lads when you said you preferred
his follow-up:

Cumberland Gap, Cumberland Gap,
Sixteen miles to the Cumberland Gap . . .

THE QUEER

He got her in just twice a year
to give the place a bottoming,
to do her best with stone-flagged floors,
mullioned, small-paned windows and
congealed fat on the iron range,
to turn the stained sagging mattress
on the brass bed where they'd all died.
But not to touch his collection
of fine, bone porcelain on the shelves.

Shuffling and dusting the photos
and other family remains,
she'd never nosed out anything
outside solitude. Nothing more
than official mail or the odd
invoice from antique shops somewhere
down near Plymouth, or Manchester.

In a tight valley where they said
it was a good man who knew
his father and everybody
knew who was having who, he was
queer. With his monthly shopping, he
took the village sneers and whispers
like the blank north wall of his house
soaking up the weather. In the Fleece,
they joked of what he did with sheep
and the postman, scoured the cleaner
for gossip. But she only saw
the camouflage of the hump-backed
ex-army jacket bagged-up round
the middle with old baler twine
lugging hay towards the cowsheds
as she flayed the threadbare rugs. And
when he dropped her from the tractor
at the foot of the steep dirt track,
she never had an inkling what
the grimly gay smile was wanting

or that it concealed the navy
captain's wife, the horn-rimmed dealer's
widow from Harrogate, the York
spinster and , more recently, the
slim young cellist from the Hallé.

WOMAN'S HOURS

She fears the empty, coming evening
when echoes of playgroup songs
and the squeak of pushchair wheels
will overpower soap opera theme tunes,
will tell her there was something there
as they pulse from beneath the sterile ground
across the table from where the kids
have left for university and him
for the woman under thirty.

She will try to dope the memory
with a double anything,
tell herself he wasn't any good at it,
might reflect on the Woman's Hour
woman intoning the new start, confidence —
no mention of exhaustion, waste.

She will return to action's zero point —
the sitting, the sitting —
around which the sounds circle,
sometimes slowly, sometimes fast.
Occasionally, she will be drawn out,
flung off dizzy to search for another
fanciable body, then pulled back
to walk the winter garden where
for months a spade has been left
sunk in a neglected bed.

BOON AND MILLS

These things happen. You never know
who you'll meet, what you'll do if it
gets as far as a brush of hands
or a look that makes you tremble
like the first time, when you know you'll
miss some one before they've gone. They
will say that the real thing only
happens once. But these things happen —

maybe on a train. Like them. Her
to mother's — and a few days off. Him
returning from a conference.
He had found it easy to ask,
then to take more business trips. And
her to get away to mother's.
Year of heart's heat, blindness, sweetness
more intense than lies, guilt. Then they
tried to stop, pretended to be
just friends. But there was something there
not weak enough to be restrained.

They met again, walked by the firs
on Chunal Moor. For the first time
there were silences, the kind they
knew — of indifference, marriage.
A strange relief. Of course, they
had known they couldn't — him with two, her
with three: too much hurt to spread. The
impossible union. She would
drop him off and that would be that,
joked: 'Reason stronger than desire?'

Then eyes had pinned him to a cloud,
hair had smelled of flowered heather . . .

They watched the grass-prints fade on skin.

Swooping down to Glossop station,
when she cried he couldn't even hold
her hand, was dumb as the future
where neither risked the danger of
a call or letter, where both watched
feeling condense to memory,
life grow tinier in the mist
of the rear-view mirror,
waiting for the lost excitement
of the unattended moment.

MURDO

They used four bullets. Took everything.

What's to live for you'd wondered
when you called. Or rather when you left him,
watched you erase him with a wave
then disappear in a cloud of red
as the Rover churned the dusty *murram* road.

He'd be sitting alone outside his tent
on a folding canvas chair under the *mvule* tree,
breakfast glass of beer on the old tin box
where he kept a thousand pounds in change
to hand across the cotton scales he'd rigged again.
Singing along to an air on the wind-up gramophone,
with the good eye left from Arnhem
he'd scan the plain for the first Alur or Kakwa
to break the haze, would count the bobbing bales.
Then days, years of weighing, counting. And
nights remembering the tug of salmon on the Tweed.

He slept alone on top of the box
since Ojok's brothers beat him up, warned him off —
though there'd been a missionary some time after.
But love hung dead behind cracked glass
on a pole beside his pillow —
after the war there'd been this boy in Kelso.
When he got too keen, the Borders
were not big enough to hide them
nor, when the family knew, Edinburgh even,
had driven them here where fever took . . .
It all came out when drunk on a shoot with talk
of going back. But he drank away all leave
in Entebbe, gossiped with the other buyers.

When I'd called to warn him of the rising,
he laughed and said he lived
beneath the vulture's eye
then poured another malt and put on
Peggy Lee and *Is That All There Is?*

LIFE CLASS

In two years,
the pain fades, he read.
And occupy the mind.
He has tried
local history
and carpentry.
This autumn, he colours
the model's tan,
marks the lines
around the eyes.
Not like her, skin
perfect till sixty.
Just the mole on her chin -
a piece of pure white paper
with a corner bent over.
He draws her, even
into landscapes.
'Good', the tutor says.
'Draw what you want.'
But a nude was rejected
for the exhibition.
Though done from memory,
too explicit they said.

Still-life next week.
On the polished table,
the first thing they bought,
he will lay out
her only shimmering dress,
an opened bottle of wine
with two glasses
and a vase of irises,
her favourite flowers.

A FLOOD

For two days

it

rained puddles
(the little one said)
and left the lawn sodden,
the soil waiting for the rock
to sponge its water
into the river's spate

kept the children to the attic
where they saw the brown stain
grow on the ceiling
then the steady drip
from beneath the purlin

peat-stained tapwater
with moorland run-off

kept us long together
by the streaming windows,
trapped us again
into that first time
when eyes affirmed,
touch ached

washed away the difficulties
when the spring sun flowered
casual thoughts
of what else, other.

MISSIONARY

Bald, erect and very red,
not long docked from Grand Bassam,
up there he fills us with the message . . .

'And for speakers of Dida, Attie, Agni,
Mr, Balmer's *Catechism* and *Law of the Friend*
have been translated and St. Mark is on the way.
At Akoupé, the bamboo and matting church
has been completed. Now they have nothing else:
gone the snake-temple and fetich house.
Gone too old dances where women bared themselves.
Yes, the stony ground is broken, fertile.
Moulding the lives of ignorant people,
God now comes before the devil dares.
So give up your mite that the work may continue.
In the name of Him, Amen.'

As the boxes are passed around
and the piles of silver mount,
a back-row boy licks the stub of a pencil
then inside a hymn-book puts,

RS did Sandra Bailey
behind the chapel lavatories.
This is very true.

Up above,
there are only bats
watching

the treasurer in the vestry,
fiddling the books, pocketing the balance,
singing quietly to himself,

'. . . how she cried
as she tried
my banana . . .'

SOUTINE

Chaim,
    It arrived yesterday.
Do you know what my friends
are saying about you?
They say you make everything
evil. Not look evil.
It isn't me you've painted.
You've turned me into paint.
True, you've caught me at
a violent moment.
Or have you caught all my
violence? But that's all
of us, isn't it? I could
be anybody. So
it seems pointless to say,
think anything about
the likeness. I only
see the way your paint twists
my mouth, the blubbery
fatness of the paint. You
have put my churning gut
on my lips. And I can't
even remember who
or what I was hating
at the time. The content
of my face is there but
in complete distortion.
Does my hair stiffen and
angle as in a gale,
do my eyes rear up — who
am I to say if it
is good or not? Or will
it ever hang next to
Rembrandt? Does it bother
you? Robert doubts it. He
says it is in no way
me you've done, but yourself.
That you have taken me

over, have opened the
sluices of self as far
as they can be raised, that
the complete expression
of your own feelings is
all that matters. He says
you are indifferent to
whether or not I should
pay you? Your poverty
says so. But you must be
what I want. Better this
for us than be like some
good technician touching —
up what people want for
a small, chic gallery.
Rather I lie facing
the wall in a room or
as a rough mark in an
unseen sketchbook I think.
I am writing because
the ox-carcass might still
hang in your studio.
I couldn't stand the rotting
stench of one more visit
if it is. So I'll send
your fee in a few days.

Monique tells me you're off
to the Pyrenees soon.
I wonder what you'll do
to those untouched landscapes.
No doubt you'll cover them
with thick, exciting paint,
will eliminate all
that we expect and show
nature's convulsions just
as you show all of ours.
I can't wait to see them.

SICILIAN BUTTERCUPS

Bad layers. Useless.
But Christ, to look at —
the comb, its two leaves meeting,
the spikes stood up all round,
the centre hollow as a crown.
And yellow. That yellow
yellower than their names.

He'd sit for hours
inside the pen,
watching them strut about,
picking out the ones to show,
muttering softly: 'Handsome. Grand.'
And once: 'Look at them!
Just like a swaying meadow.'

When fifty pounds was a lot of money,
she thought the win would buy
them all a holiday, some clothes.
Perhaps new curtains.
Instead, he bought another cote,
five more pairs —
and a cabinet for the cup.

And always the stink
of his shit-clagged boots in the hall.
And always her quiet brooding
on what meant more than she did
as she rocked her last to sleep,
nursed hate and a dream
of flight from the cold nest.

PURE RESEARCH

He has progressed
from lefthandedness
and righthandedness
in mice to studying
the movement patterns
of a snake's head.
This is a collaboration
at the Sorbonne, Paris:
a term each year.
A professor, his teaching
is in Toronto where
each night he buys himself
a bottle of brandy
then drives ten miles
to the cabin they built
on the edge of the forest.
In his absence, she
has taught herself batik
and other techniques
of surface pattern.
She has started to sell.
By midnight, she sleeps
while he, awake, tries
to discover just why
she wants to leave him.

ZENNYBODYEVERTOLDYAYALOOKLIKEELVISPRESLEY

Weather-forecasters should be drowned:
we never saw the dale through pressure
low as the huddles of drenched fleeces;
a landscape four feet high and up there,
somewhere, Ingleborough where we came
to find a burn in touch again.

The lounge fire dried us out
and farmer's lads who'd somehow crazy
plunged through mist in dented cars
to drink like mad to speechlessness.

'ZennybodyevertoldyayalooklikeElvisPresley'
from a shepherd's girl cracked us open,
rolled us achingly together before

the sounds below of heartbreak hotel
recovering - a mop-bucket handle clank,
clink of empty bottles being crated.

And later, filling our silence,
the engine whined up the difficult road
towards the plateau top
above the blash on the windscreen
of the slowly sobering rain.

THE BOY IN YOU

1. Waking Up

Blind in freezing darkness,
an order of sounds unchanging
programmed winter mornings.

Each day switched on at six
to the creaking handle of their bedroom door;
her cat-like padding slippers down the stairs;
the rooting for sticks and scrape of shovel
under coal; the draw-tin roaring the fire,
drowning shipping forecast.

Through the wall, his work of getting going
began - coughs nail-sharp, gasps on asthma pump,
like bellows filling lungs enough to knock, call.

But always lay
till first light shaped the curtain-rings.
Then the scuffle round for books, coat,
bolted food and into the lane
to see him standing half-way up the bank,
bag of tools and snap diagonal across his back,
heaving to the wheeze of the pump.

And every day the hammer pounded out —
this can't be right, this can't be right.
And when the chauffered Bentley glided past,

mad-eyed, I made it disappear.

2. The Boy In You

As a boy, John, you lay alone for long sumer days
belly-flat on the bank of the slow Spink Brook
with brain-deep eye peering at the stone
patient for the stickleback to nose,

first the eyes which knew you were there then
the blue-black back and blazing scarlet belly.
Hands in. Cupped. Gently under. Splash.
And you wondered in the flash of his disappearance
what he knew, wanted and why he lived
at all.
Years on, your vision tried to catch the people
hiding under stones of circumstance in fast cities,
looking for their souls to show
so that you could discover
how they lived, for what
and why they kept hurtling so busily
towards the fires which they knew were there.

3. **Past Present**

There is the skrike of a crow
in Hugh Proctor's sycamore
and an all-clear siren
after the boom of blasting
in distant Biddulph quarry.
There is the clank of a bucket
from Chaddock's cowshed and
the voice of a girl who talks of the future
hugged up tight on Bailey's Hill.
Butty Wood below the juncus-pocked pasture
lies still in the late summer stillness.
And along the stony lane
a tractor rattles from mowing
past two old men who cough out the past,
say no to the rising bungalows.
But the boy in the hug says yes to it all
and longs for the unknown world.
Thirty years on
the boy returned worn out by it all
and found the sycamore axed,
the quarry worked out and
a scrapyard for derelict cars,

the pasture swallowed by culs-de-sac,
the cowshed converted to residential,
the hayfield grazed bare by railed-in ponies,
the lane under tarmac,
the old men under headstones,
the stile to the wood hedged with barbed wire.
And himself desiring Bailey's Hill.

4. Dick

Silent before his wife,
he returned no word to the accusation
thinking only of the sentence
and shaking
like the night he lay in bed
with his parents' muffled shouts
thudding louder and louder into plasterboard.
He knew all this
so what could he say to people who thought
that a man of sixty was at fault?
Things had just happened, gone on
even though he had said to his lover
over and over,
'Go away, go far away and wait —
for death or something.
You've maddened my brain
with the gift of your words and body:
it'll lead to something terrible.'
And just as he feared, here he stood.
Until the trembling stopped
and he realised
that he had never wanted either of them,
any of those years, wanted
only the missing ease and quiet before it all,
of loneliness at its very best
like on that cold morning
when he had run from the blazing row
to the far meadow and flung himself
face down to join his tears with the wet grass.

BUILDING THE PALACE OF DREAMS

The brickies built as if the craze
would die tomorrow: no windows
made it easy work. They would raise
the scaffolding every day. No
time for safety rails or union
men, till planking shifted. Below,
they stared at the hodman as he
hung like Harold Lloyd before his
scream split the new-laid boards where the
joiners were making the stage. Three
years in plaster humped his spine, made
a leg stiff as a pole. Then she
left: he could not do it any
more. Now, leg down aisle, he dreams of
running The Yellow Brick Road — many
times before the final credits
plunges, yelling for the exit.

AFTER THE FIGHT AT THE PICKET

(*after Robert Payne*)

All day you could hear the noise beyond the slag-heap -
surging and dying roars; screams; horses squealing
like abattoired pigs; orders, speeches through megaphones;
trucks revving through the cordon. And then the quiet

of exhaustion. Only the empty children's swings
creaking in the breeze broke the stillness. Then I saw it,
the wounded pigeon flapping down over the tip, coming
slowly out of the sky chased by the cloud of crows.

It settled on the roof of the Club. The crows followed,
perched there, watching the pigeon, waiting for it to die.
It stayed still, head buried in its shoulders,
grey and blue feathers unmoving in the strong sunlight.

There was magnificence in the pigeon — in the spread
of its limp, grey feathers, in its silence and seclusion,
its dignity, its uninterrupted contemplation of itself,
utterly careless of the presence of the thirty crows.

The crows cawed loudly, strutting the ridge as if they
owned the roof, craning short ugly necks, puffing out
black chests. And when they saw the faintest movement
of its wings, the crows noticed the tiredness, stiffened.

They watched preening themselves, sharpening beaks on slate,
filling the air with screams until it came — a single, slow
movement, an attempt to fly which failed. And they came down,
flying one after the other, screaming, clapping their wings,

pecking at head, eyes and soft places among feathers. Still
the pigeon kept silent, but twitching, flinging its head
around then quickly burying it again, enclosed within itself,
tranquil, clamped to the roof. Then the crows were silent,

seemed afraid, hardly daring to scream. Lowering sunlight
turned blue feathers to gold and I could see it quivering,
tense, edging quietly towards the gable for easy flight.
An hour. Nothing. Then the sudden furious screaming,

pecking, black wings opening like fans. Three times, always
in groups, digging beaks deep, knifing it to spasms of pain.
Stillness again until at last it reached the edge, gathered
its strength, flapped slowly away. The crows followed.

It made it to the nearby silver birches. Soon a tree
was leafed with black feathers, shook. The din of death
was awful, even echoed when they'd finished. One by one
they headed for the valley beyond the tip, ready for

tomorrow's trouble. Below them, groups of women scavenged
for scraps of coal. Miners straggled back across the playground,
discussed what next. A pigeon landed on the see-saw. The baby
woke up. I pushed for home, planning her future.

REPETITION IS THE DEATH OF US THEY SAY

Saturday morning. They shout
at each other again about
who should take the boys
to the park: nothing really.
Later, goalposts. They play
penalties. The rain-softened clay
would take a stud he thinks
and of being single again . . .
weak sun. Blown leaves. That time of year.
The first match. New strip. A clear
run on goal . . . He shows the boys
heading. One wants a hug. Then the other.
He wishes and loves simultaneously.
The sheer impossibiliy.
So we switch between the two.
Back home, she shouts at him
to turn the volume down.
He is watching the results. Town
have lost. And he is twenty again,
in the team van where they exaggerate
old scores and brag
about how good they shag,
how many, how many
times: 'It's what women need,'
Dropped off, he sees his mother
sitting in the parlour
telling his sister the facts
without the what goes on,
invoking the sheer impossible:
true love; to be sensible;
save it for the right man;
the good marriage.
And him in this state,
wondering if it's too late
or early. And how many times
would he think of all this.

THE LONGING

Last time I stayed in New Orleans
got stupid drunk in Walt's Lounge, met
an Indian woman who told
of nineteen years growing up Crow
in Wolf Point. It sounded like hell
trapped on the reservation. But
when her lips gave out 'Montana'
then painted the Big Sky State, just
left of the Rocky Mountains where
the slow Bitteroot meanders
into the Blackfoot River, wow,
I had to go there fast.
                       Never
made it. But now when things explode
over decorating or I
miss the coal man, haul filthy sacks
down fifteen steps to far cellars,
when winter days never lighten
or mortgage rates go up again
or just when the drink-glow hits,
there it is, that mouth, opening
to shape the word, that needed lift,
opening like a wide exit.

THE GOSPEL TENT, NEW ORLEANS JAZZFEST, 1978

Backstage, the Smooth Family of Slidell,
next on, panic to find the eldest daughter.
Slugging whisky, the father stumbles questions
amongst the giggling Gospel Choralettes of Metairie.
But she is out of the flap in a Pontiac
with Homer, drummer with Brother Billy Blind Boy,
bouncing to the spirituals of God's Chosen Few
whose leader is on a holy-roller — on his back
riffing out a never-ending climax, the sweating
congregation a sway of clapping. In the performer's lot,
humming to the distant din, in their chrome-finned bus
the Voices of Revelation slide into wine-stained,
white satin stage suits, look down and smile
at the top of the rocking car. And some one says
what great things you can see from on high.

ARE MADE OF THIS

Spacing themselves out
to the same thing for days on end —
an office choked by memos,
bills you must get round to paying

or hit you after years
with the scent of bluebells
on a nature table
or the why, why, why
of why they could not
make your Auntie Annie better

or haunt with spitting faces
as you try to put things right
canvassing the slam-door, leafy suburbs

or give back the moment
the night something told
that just before you snuff it
there will be this second of calm
like the stillness of the market square
on a warm summer's evening
between shop-shut and dusk

or haul you back
to a smirk in a graduation gown
when, like too many others,
you forgot you came from street-dust
with only your parents,
faces pushed out of shot,
knowing the real achievement

or corner your reflection
in the black-framed snap
of grey-haired spirits in bombazine skirts,
who doled out chocolate once a year,
and unsmiling, starch-necked men
with noses to match your own

or taunt with the one
you see just once a week
but think of twenty times a day
and may never cuddle in a soft bed
or trap you time and again
into trying to make some sense of it all.

THE USHERETTE

She valued the past in one-and-nines
and two-and-sixes, held a torch for
black and white shots of Errol Flynn and
Clark Gable, rescued from the foyer
when they shut the Roxy, her only
lovers since the Somme had taken him.
It took a large sherry to release
the pictures, to say how handsome he
looked between them. And you saw it was
his frame which was polished with starshine.

A CURSE FOR THE MAN WHO CAME TO DINNER

I put him up, a favour for a friend,
held his hand through a rough time,
watched him recover to his normal self -
always scratching his arms and hair,
complaining about the texture of chick peas,
burning my fire long into the early morning
while endlessly playing his favourite track:
Russ Russell and the Rustlers doing
O Lord It's Hard To Be Humble. And
rising at noon. The gas bill did it.

'I'm a night person you see.' he explained.
I suggested Anchorage, Alaska where
no doubt he could easily avoid
the mean three hours of winter daylight,
where seal meat permanently furs the tongue,
where country and western singers get lynched
and the state bird is the mosquito.

OCCUPATIONAL THERAPY

'The lifting and putting down of a glass
is all the work I want,' Ray said. Not that
he couldn't see the good sense of being kept

busy all day, like when they'd tried to dry
him out. Taking the mind off things always
was important. Like drink. And that still helped.

But woodwork. 'So help me, you know that I'm
to joinery what Hitler was to peace
and this girl says would you like to make me

a nestle of tables Mr. Grocott.
They have these kits. And they made me do it.
This girl says very good Mr. Grocott.

I says no it isn't, it's bloody awful.'
He lifted his pint, watched the sun sink through
the glass door, yelled, 'Christ, see that. Same again.'

IN THE BREAKS BETWEEN BINGO

John Love was in fine form
soloing around Kid Howard licks
then taking them into his own.
Nobody listened much
but we thought they liked us here
until after *After You've Gone*
a drunk the size of Yorkshire
told the clarinet he had a tone
like a cat pissing in a biscuit tin,
the bass that he sounded like his granny
thwacking dust from a hung-out rug,
that he'd come here to drink
and if he wanted tunes,
he'd shove ten pee in the trumpet's gob
and press his belly-button.

Salesman, banjo, Arthur Bladder
(who liked his name and had a printed card —
Can Hold His Own In Any Conversation)
tried to reason:
'We're only trying to do our job . . .'

'What have premature ejaculation
and a banjo solo got in common?'
yelled Yorkshire, delivered,
'You know it's coming
but can't do owt about it.'
And they laughed and clapped him.

Mute, we cased our horns
in the only silence sure to gag a heckler,
the one they gave to the bingo-caller,
then watched the British Legion
biro out its numbers, the coloured balls
flirting with all luck:
'On its own, number . . .' And John
looked down, fingered the folded cheque,
invented a hum inside his head,
remembered the bounce of jazz clubs and
Doreen naked under her duffel coat
and when it all was fun.

LIGHTS WHICH DON'T GO OUT

She kisses and tells me
Angela Smith is not dead
and the thought shoots me
into wet lips in midge-loaded darkness
on Severn banks, her downy arms

like those on the women we wanted
as kids, following their strapless tops
and bum-crack shorts down seaside proms

and later peeped at through net curtains
before choosing one for a paid-for,
stone-faced, dry-bonk in a damp room
just to get the badge, the manhood tag,
release the dream of undressing
bred the first time I saw Jenny Agutter
flitting nude across the screen
in *Walkabout*, clean, smooth and decent,
a pure woman's skin, a million steps from

the roughness of the hands of the man
who touched me up when I was seven
or the burnt flesh of Chelsea Ron
in a bedsit fire through falling asleep
with a naked bulb and flickering closedown
on a burst sofa with a fag dangling
from lips no one had kissed since childhood,
his mates in the pub blaming dope
and how one thing had led to another

like this I've-missed-you-hug
from someone fairly new on a cold night
ribboning out this past and telling me
that even if I think it has or might
nothing will ever really go away —
the body-bag is see-through, and luminous.

THE WIRE-COATHANGER STORY

'You always look knackered these days.'

Well you try sagging around for years under
your grandfather's overcoat, Methodism etc.
You try seeing what it's like
kept in the dark, taken out just
twice a year: once back to your birthplace,
the cleaners, before the inevitable funeral.
Then back to the hanging, the upright coffin
with the weight of family, the past
on your shoulders. Responsibility.
You try shaking it off even if you know
you were made, meant for something lighter,
different. What fits? Anything?
But does it, did it ever work like that?

I mean, always getting the wrong partner,
I moved from bedsit to bedsit
drip-drying nylon shirts over stained baths.
Got lucky, or so I thought, when yanked out
with a jangle from a tangle of others
in a wardrobe bottom. You could say
I was sort of rescued to this
via two spells of daylight — one,
fun at first before ages bored to death
carrying a lightweight business suit
swaying in the back of a Vauxhall Cavalier.
From there, not sure how, it was
seven years as a TV aerial
hung from an attic window in Handsworth.
The things I saw from up there changed everything.
Black and white. Hate. The futility of hope.
(You can get like that you know).
Years bury. I'd have gladly accepted the scrapheap
when the box conked out but got reshaped
in an emergency to fish a ring from a toilet.
Stayed like that quite a while, on a hook,
taken down to unblock the occasional drain.

Suddenly she left leaving me for dead
in the airing cupboard. The new woman
must have been desperate, straightened me out.
Ten years later, I'm trapped into this.
Sometimes you wish yourself back
in the wireworks, the machine drawing you out
in a pure straight line. The possibilities.
But like I said . . .
And when you think what you've been through
what I've learned is that in spite of the moaning,
this is it. And it could be worse. I mean, my mate
spends his life twisted into a perpetual paint-stirrer
for the D I Yife. So maybe always looking knackered's
a small price and . . .

Hang about, look at that for a piece of skirt!

STAMPS

Too many times I've licked
the back of her head,
though necessarily so.
Bad enough, but now
we get the hangers-on,
the special issues.
Millions love it:
lick, lick, lick —
arseholes, feet.
Not me. I try to be
a revolution —
kick, kick, kick,
stamp, stamp, stamp.

John Lancaster was born in Biddulph, Stoke-on-Trent, in 1946. He has lived in Sheffield, Manchester, Birmingham, New Orleans and Huddersfield, where he works as a part-time lecturer and tutor for the University, and for the Open College of the Arts.